D1604723

MODERN WEAPONS
COMPARED AND CONTRASTED

ARMORED
FIGHTING
VEHICLES

MARTIN J. DOUGHERTY

rosen publishing's
rosen
central®

New York

This edition first published in 2013 by:

The Rosen Publishing Group, Inc.
29 East 21st Street
New York, NY 10010

Additional end matter copyright © 2013 by The Rosen Publishing Group, Inc.

Library of Congress Cataloging-in-Publication Data

Dougherty, Martin J.
Armored fighting vehicles/Martin J. Dougherty.
   p. cm.—(Modern weapons: compared and contrasted)
Includes bibliographical references and index.
ISBN 978-1-4488-9244-0 (library binding)
1. Armored vehicles, Military I. Title.
UG446.5.D6268 2013
623.74'75—dc23

2012033096

Manufactured in the United States of America

CPSIA Compliance Information: Batch #W13YA: For further information, contact Rosen Publishing, New York, New York, at 1-800-237-9932.

Copyright © 2012 by Amber Books Ltd. First published in 2012 by Amber Books Ltd.

Contents

Introduction

Combat vehicles primarily exist to provide mobility and protection to a weapons system or to a group of troops. They have revolutionized warfare, making it possible to launch high-speed breakthrough-and-exploitation attacks and to counter them. Where previously the battle front moved at the speed of a marching man, today's mechanized forces are capable of dominating a huge area, often surprising opposing forces by appearing where they are least expected.

New designs of armored vehicles have appeared to fill an ever-increasing number of niches. Armored fighting vehicles (tanks) directly engage the enemy with powerful guns, while infantry fighting vehicles carry and support infantry forces. These expensive, top-end assets are supported by lighter reconnaissance, transport and specialist vehicles. Striking the right balance between capability and affordability is a tricky business; sometimes it is necessary to accept a lower level of capability in order to afford enough vehicles to fully equip a nation's armed forces.

LEFT: A German Leopard 2 main battle tank splashes through water during exercises. The Leopard 2 is in service with a number of European countries, including Denmark and Austria.

CHAPTER 1
Gulf War 1991: Main Battle Tanks 1

Armor Protection: Turret and Hull

▶ **T-55**
▶ **T-72A**
▶ **M1A1 Abrams**
▶ **AMX-30**

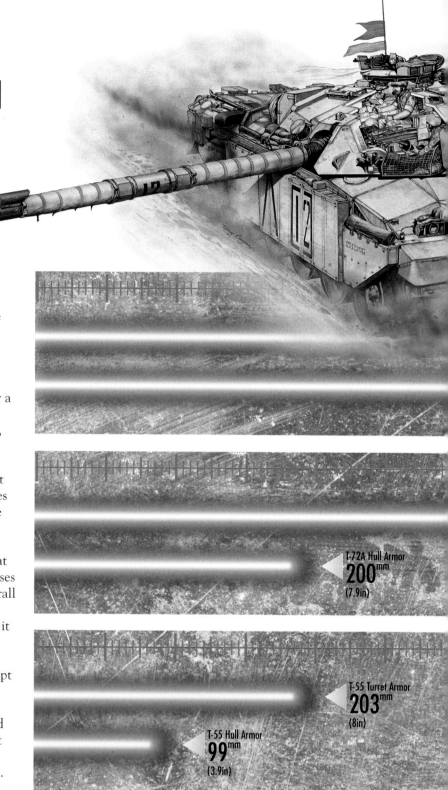

The armored fighting vehicles (AFVs) of the 1991 Gulf War were the product of a long contest between weapons and protection. Each advance in armor technology was inevitably matched by a weapon that could defeat it. Armoring tanks in ever-thicker steel worked for a time, but there is a limit to how much weight a tank can carry. Greater efficiency was necessary, and this came from two sources – improved materials and better shaping.

Sloped or curved armor creates a chance that an incoming round will glance off, and increases the effective thickness of the armor, even if the round does punch in. A round that arrives at a 90-degree angle to the armor will have to penetrate a much shorter distance than one that comes in at an acute angle. Composite armor uses layers of different materials to increase the overall effectiveness of the armor. It is hard to cast composite armor in anything but flat slabs, but it is still sloped for increased protection.

It is simply not possible to make a tank invulnerable from all angles, so designers attempt to maximize protection against the most likely threats. In a conventional tank-vs-tank action, most incoming fire will strike the hull front and the turret. However, experience has shown that a threat can come from anywhere, especially when tanks are operating in close urban terrain. Tank armor is often a compromise between reasonable all-round protection and the ability to defeat a top-end armor-piercing warhead from at least some angles.

Armor Protection

Due to intervening obstacles, the turret is often the only part of a tank that can be hit, especially at long range. Not surprisingly, it is often the most heavily armored part of the vehicle, but this cannot be taken to extremes. Tanks likely to be engaged at short range need a well-armored hull if they are to survive the encounter. Armor is only one aspect of a tank's protection; mobility is another. A tank that is so heavily weighed down by its armor that it cannot move quickly may actually be more vulnerable than a much lighter vehicle.

T-72A Hull Armor
200mm
(7.9in)

T-55 Turret Armor
203mm
(8in)

T-55 Hull Armor
99mm
(3.9in)

AMX-30 Turret Armor
80mm
(3.15in)

AMX-30 Hull Armor
79mm
(3.1in)

6

1 The flat planes of armor presented by these M1 Abrams tanks are characteristic of composite armor. The turret and front hull armor is well sloped to give the tank maximum protection. The hull sides and rear are more vulnerable to attack.

1

M1A1 Abrams Turret Armor
600mm
(23.6in)

M1A1 Abrams Hull Armor
600mm
(23.6in)

M1A1 Abrams

T-72A Turret Armor
560mm
(22in)

T-72A

T-55

TOP LEFT: The armored protection of the British Challenger I tank is classified, but in combat has proved to be as effective as that of the M1A1 Abrams.

AMX-30

CHAPTER 2

Gulf War 1991: Main Battle Tanks 2

Main Gun Range and Caliber

▶ **T-55**
▶ **T-72A**
▶ **M1A1 Abrams**
▶ **Challenger 1**
▶ **AMX-30**

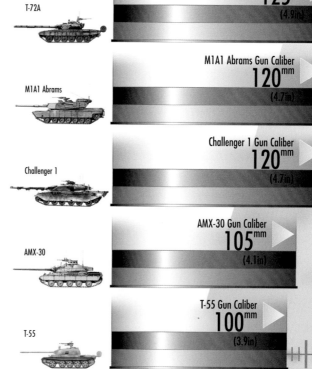

The ability to hit the target at a great distance grants a tank both offensive and defensive advantages. Offensively, a long-range weapon enables the tank to dominate a larger part of the battle area and to hit targets it cannot approach. Defensively, it improves survivability – if a tank force can engage beyond its enemies' effective range, then the battle can be very one-sided. A tank's gun has to be powerful enough to penetrate the armor of a rival main battle tank (MBT) and to destroy any other target it is turned against. This requires a large, powerful shell. However, big shells take up a lot of space, which limits the number that can be carried. A lighter gun with more ammunition might seem like a good trade-off. Up to a point it might be, but a gun that is too light to penetrate an enemy tank is useless. Modern MBTs are rarely armed with weapons under 100mm (3.9in) in caliber; with anything lighter it may not matter whether or not a hit is scored.

Main Gun Caliber

Tank gun calibers have remained standardized in the 100–125mm (3.9–4.9in) range for several decades. These guns offer an excellent compromise between range, hitting power and ammunition capacity.

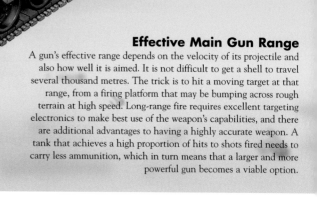

ABOVE: A main battle tank's gun is to a great extent its reason for existing. As shown in this illustration of the M1A1, it is a large and complex piece of equipment that must be loaded, aimed and stabilized from within the turret. The gun's breech takes up much of the front of the turret, with ammunition stowed in the rear. The crew and all other systems must fit into whatever space is left over.

Effective Main Gun Range

A gun's effective range depends on the velocity of its projectile and also how well it is aimed. It is not difficult to get a shell to travel several thousand metres. The trick is to hit a moving target at that range, from a firing platform that may be bumping across rough terrain at high speed. Long-range fire requires excellent targeting electronics to make best use of the weapon's capabilities, and there are additional advantages to having a highly accurate weapon. A tank that achieves a high proportion of hits to shots fired needs to carry less ammunition, which in turn means that a larger and more powerful gun becomes a viable option.

1A1 Abrams Gun Range
3000m
(3749yd)

Challenger 1 Gun Range
3000m
(3281yd)

T-72A Gun Range
2000m
(2187yd)

T-55 Gun Range
1500m
(1640yd)

AMX-30 Gun Range
1500m
(1640yd)

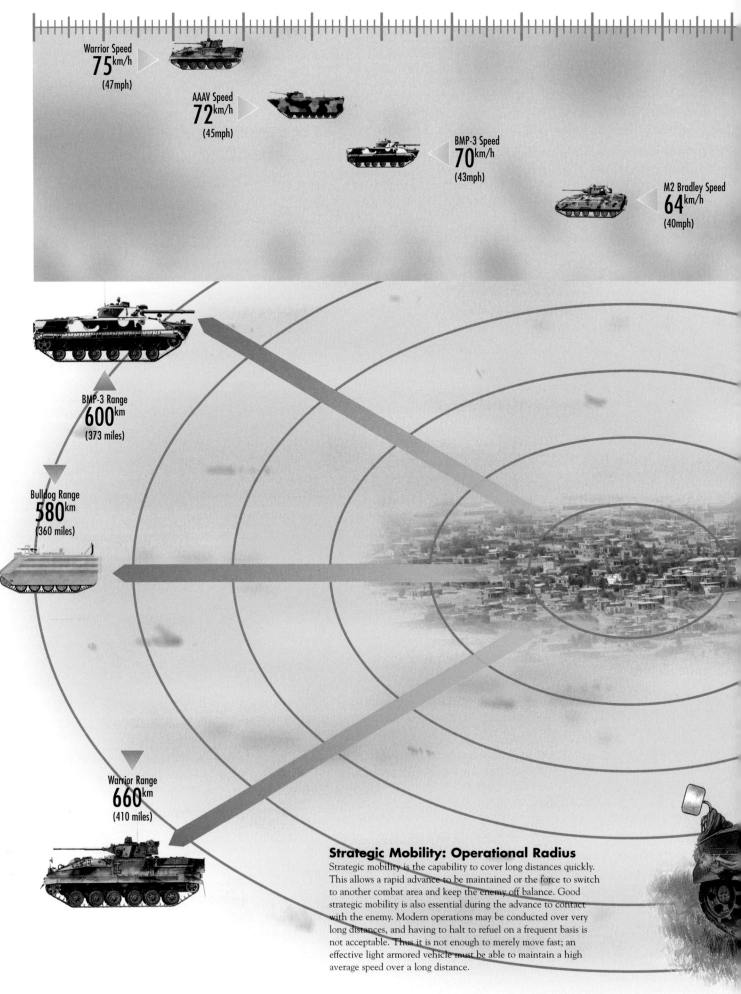

Warrior Speed
75km/h
(47mph)

AAAV Speed
72km/h
(45mph)

BMP-3 Speed
70km/h
(43mph)

M2 Bradley Speed
64km/h
(40mph)

BMP-3 Range
600km
(373 miles)

Bulldog Range
580km
(360 miles)

Warrior Range
660km
(410 miles)

Strategic Mobility: Operational Radius

Strategic mobility is the capability to cover long distances quickly. This allows a rapid advance to be maintained or the force to switch to another combat area and keep the enemy off balance. Good strategic mobility is also essential during the advance to contact with the enemy. Modern operations may be conducted over very long distances, and having to halt to refuel on a frequent basis is not acceptable. Thus it is not enough to merely move fast; an effective light armored vehicle must be able to maintain a high average speed over a long distance.

CHAPTER 3

Twenty-first Century Light Vehicles 1

Maximum Speed and Range

▶ **FV430 Bulldog**
▶ **M2 Bradley**
▶ **BMP-3**
▶ **Warrior**
▶ **AAAV**

Maximum Speed
Top speed is usually only attainable on a road or fairly flat ground. Racing cross-country or over obstacles is a thoroughly unpleasant experience for anyone aboard an armored vehicle, no matter how good its suspension may be. It is, however, better than being hit by enemy fire.

Bulldog Speed
52km/h
(32mph)

AAAV Range
480km
(298 miles)

M2 Bradley Range
483km
(300 miles)

Light armored vehicles are an essential part of modern warfare. Their primary function is to provide mobility to the personnel or systems they carry. Protection is a secondary, but important, consideration, and most are armed either for self-defense or to provide fire support to their troops.

Tactical mobility is the ability to operate in very rough terrain, crossing obstacles without becoming stuck. For this reason, many light armored vehicles use tracks rather than wheels. This allows close cooperation with tanks. Infantry carried aboard light armored transport are able to keep pace with the tank force and to smash through relatively light defenses without dismounting. Cross-country speed is also a form of protection. A fast-moving target is hard to hit, and since these vehicles are less well protected than tanks, they may have to rely on mobility for defense.

LEFT: As with this British Warrior, the crew of an infantry fighting vehicle (IFV) remain aboard to operate its weapons and systems while infantry (referred to as "dismounts") leave the vehicle to carry out their mission. The IFV may remain close by to provide fire support or may be given a new mission once its dismounts are delivered.

CHAPTER 4

Twenty-first Century Light Vehicles 2

Personnel Capacity and Weapons Caliber

▶ **FV430 Bulldog**
▶ **M2 Bradley**
▶ **BMP-3**
▶ **Warrior**
▶ **AAAV**

AAAV

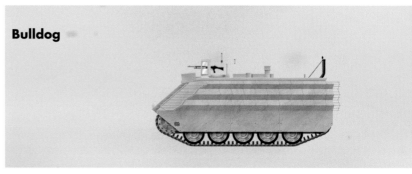
Bulldog

BMP-3

Warrior

M2 Bradley

By the time of the 1991 Gulf War, the armored personnel carrier (APC) had largely given way to the infantry fighting vehicle, moving from a "battle taxi" to a weapons platform that could support its infantry force in combat. Some older APCs mounting only a machine gun for self-defense were in use, but many of these vehicles had already been converted to other roles – for example, logistics vehicles, artillery observation vehicles, command posts, armored ambulances and platforms for a range of specialist systems such as anti-aircraft defenses.

This new generation of combat vehicle still had the same primary purpose: to provide protected transportation for an infantry force. Anti-personnel weapons that could hold up or even stop an infantry unit pose little threat to an armored vehicle. However, many lighter anti-tank weapons, which would pose no real threat to a heavily armored MBT, will easily penetrate the armor of an infantry fighting vehicle or armored personnel carrier.

To many people, anything with tracks and some sort of gun is a tank, and an infantry fighting vehicle can indeed fulfill some of a tank's functions. Its primary role is infantry support, which frees real tanks to take on major threats the IFV cannot deal with. Similarly, the weapons mounted on an infantry fighting vehicle cannot be as heavy as those in a tank's turret; there is simply no room. Indeed, any IFV design must trade off its potency as a weapons platform against its carrying capacity. If too much room is given over to weapons, the vehicle becomes essentially an ineffective and excessively vulnerable light tank with an inadequate infantry force aboard. Striking the right balance, on the other hand, creates a highly potent combined infantry/light armor force capable of dealing efficiently with a wide range of situations.

Personnel Capacity

The crew required to operate the vehicle remains fixed at two or three personnel, depending on what weapons are mounted. These personnel are necessary, so any system that takes up internal space has to be fitted at the expense of troop-carrying capacity.

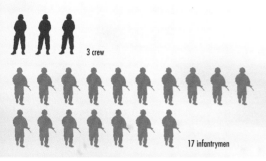

3 crew

17 infantrymen

2 crew

10 infantrymen

3 crew

7 infantrymen

3 crew

7 infantrymen

3 crew

6 infantrymen

Weapons Caliber

Most IFVs carry a machine gun for anti-personnel defense and usually a heavier weapon, such as an automatic cannon in the 20–30mm (0.79–1.2in) range, for harder targets. Some vehicles also mount anti-tank missiles.

Caliber
30mm
(1.2in)

Caliber
7.62mm
(0.3in)

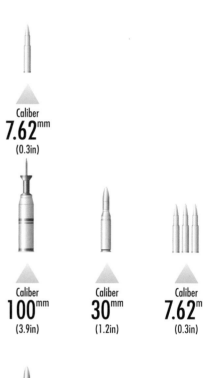

Caliber
7.62mm
(0.3in)

Caliber
100mm
(3.9in)

Caliber
30mm
(1.2in)

Caliber
7.62mm
(0.3in)

Caliber
30mm
(1.2in)

Caliber
7.62mm
(0.3in)

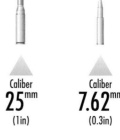

Caliber
25mm
(1in)

Caliber
7.62mm
(0.3in)

13

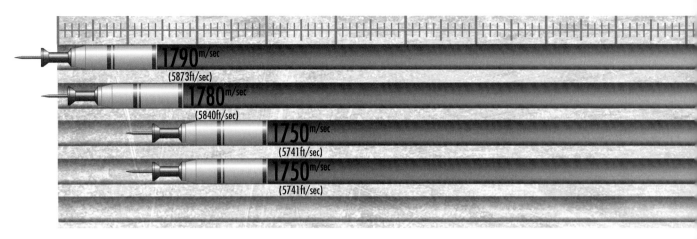

1790 m/sec
(5873ft/sec)

1780 m/sec
(5840ft/sec)

1750 m/sec
(5741ft/sec)

1750 m/sec
(5741ft/sec)

Muzzle Velocity

Modern tanks often engage at ranges of 2000–3000m (2187–3281yd). Even a projectile moving at the better part of 2000m/sec (6562ft/sec) may take a second and a half to travel from gun to target. A fast-moving tank can travel a long way in that time, reducing the chances of a hit.

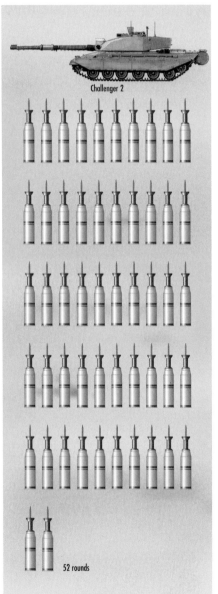

Challenger 2

52 rounds

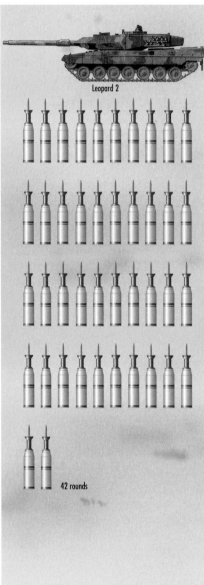

Leopard 2

42 rounds

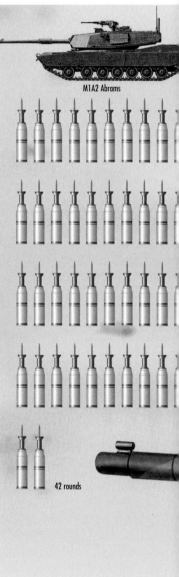

M1A2 Abrams

42 rounds

Number of Rounds

Modern armored warfare takes place at a very high tempo, with no time for ammunition resupply in the middle of a battle. Thus a tank needs to carry enough ammunition for a protracted engagement, or several short fights during a forward deployment in which it is not practicable to take on more shells.

CHAPTER 5

Main Battle Tanks Today 1

Muzzle Velocity and Number of Rounds

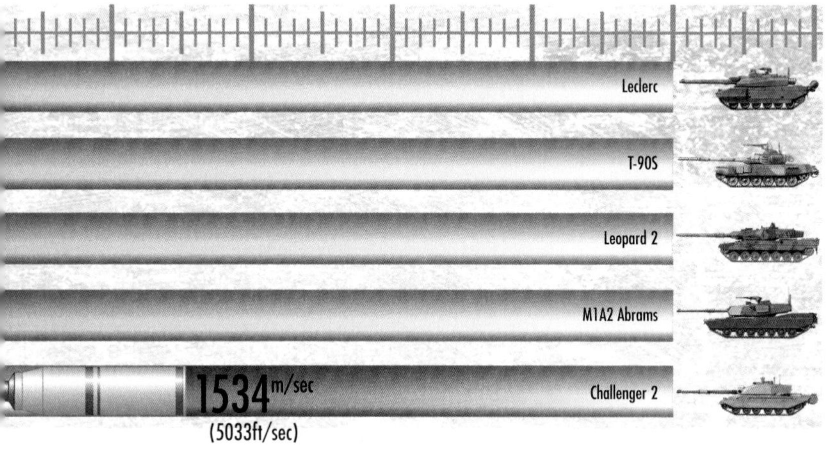

▶ **M1A2 Abrams**
▶ **Leopard 2**
▶ **T-90S**
▶ **Challenger 2**
▶ **Leclerc**

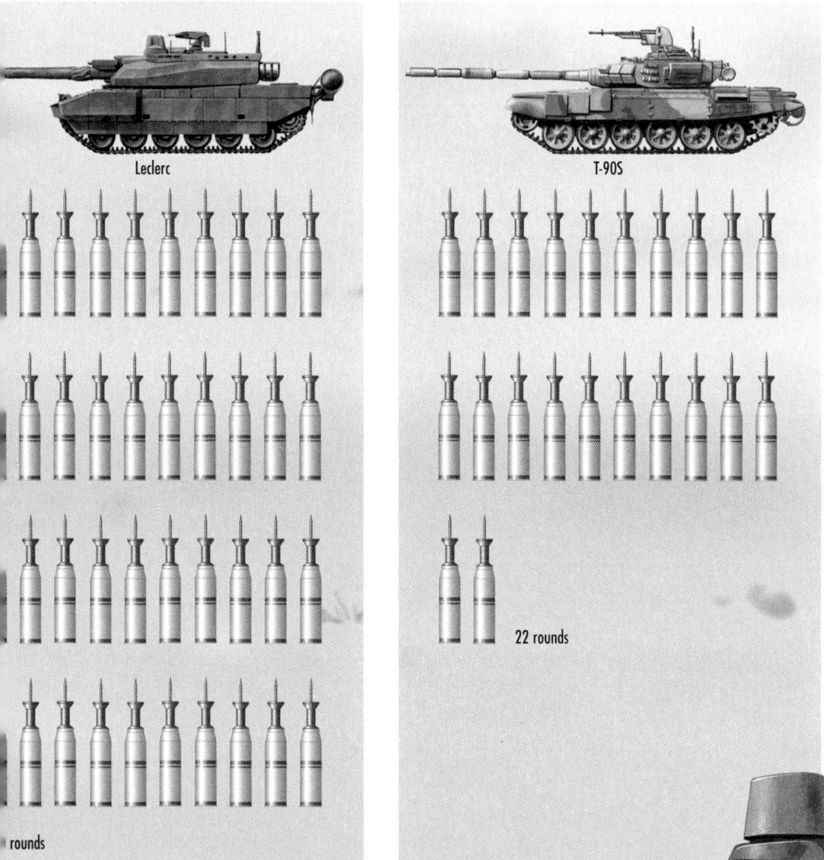

Leclerc

T-90S

Leopard 2

M1A2 Abrams

1534 m/sec
(5033ft/sec)

Challenger 2

Leclerc

T-90S

22 rounds

rounds

Modern MBTs mount a long gun capable of delivering a variety of ammunition types, each optimized to the characteristics of a different target. For anti-tank work it is most common to use an armor-piercing fin-stabilized discarding sabot (APFSDS) round, which relies for its destructive power upon impacting at high velocity. The muzzle velocity of the tank's gun is thus important in determining the penetrating power of the projectile. Shaped-charge ammunition relies less on impact velocity since its penetrative power comes from the detonation of the warhead. However, the warhead must still hit the target, and high muzzle velocity is useful here too. It equates to a flatter shell trajectory and less time between firing and hitting the target, thus reducing the chances that the target will move out of the way. Fast-moving shells are also less affected by wind, humidity and air temperature.

RIGHT: The French Leclerc main battle tank is fitted with a 120mm (4.7in) smoothbore gun. It has a theoretical rate of fire of 12 rounds per minute. If enough targets were available, a Leclerc could burn through its ready ammunition in just a few minutes of combat.

68940067

CHAPTER 6

Main Battle Tanks Today 2

Main Gun Range and Rate of Fire

▶ **M1A2 Abrams**
▶ **Leopard 2**
▶ **T-90S**
▶ **Challenger 2**
▶ **Leclerc**

Tank guns are precision weapons with a limited ammunition supply, which makes the choice of which targets to engage a critical one. Every shot must be deliberate and precise, not least because a threat that appears while the gun is being loaded cannot be engaged. Under most circumstances a tank will not shoot as fast as it can, but reloading time can nonetheless be critical. A high theoretical rate of fire means that the tank will have a shot ready soon after firing, even if that shot is not immediately taken, and contributes to the overall effectiveness of the force.

Some tanks use autoloaders to speed up the loading process, though these devices tend to be mechanically complex and have at times been plagued with malfunctions. Otherwise, the gun is loaded in the traditional manner, by the gunner and possibly another crew member manhandling a heavy shell into the breech. Even with some mechanical assistance, this requires considerable strength, especially when working in the small and awkwardly shaped space of a tank's turret.

Ammunition is usually stored at the rear of the turret, in a compartment designed to protect the crew if the ammunition is detonated by a direct hit. Rapid fire is a test of the crew's endurance; hauling shells from storage to breech will tire the crew quickly and cause the tank's rate of fire to drop off. Good design makes the reloading process as easy as possible and reduces crew fatigue, as does firing at a measured and deliberate rate.

Rate of Fire
Rate of fire is usually more important in terms of reducing the time spent without a ready shot, rather than the ability to get rid of large amounts of ammunition. Of course, in a target-rich or desperate situation, the tank will be firing as fast as it can reload and a high rate of fire may be a big advantage.

Main Gun Range
Most tank guns can throw a shell farther than their listed effective range, but the chances of a hit are minimal. There is no point in wasting ammunition in this manner; harassing fire is best left to the artillery.

M1A2 Abrams Gun Range
8000ᵐ (8749yd)

Leclerc Gun Range
4000ᵐ (4374yd)

Leclerc Rate of Fire
12
shots per minute

M1A2 Abrams Rate of Fire
10
shots per minute

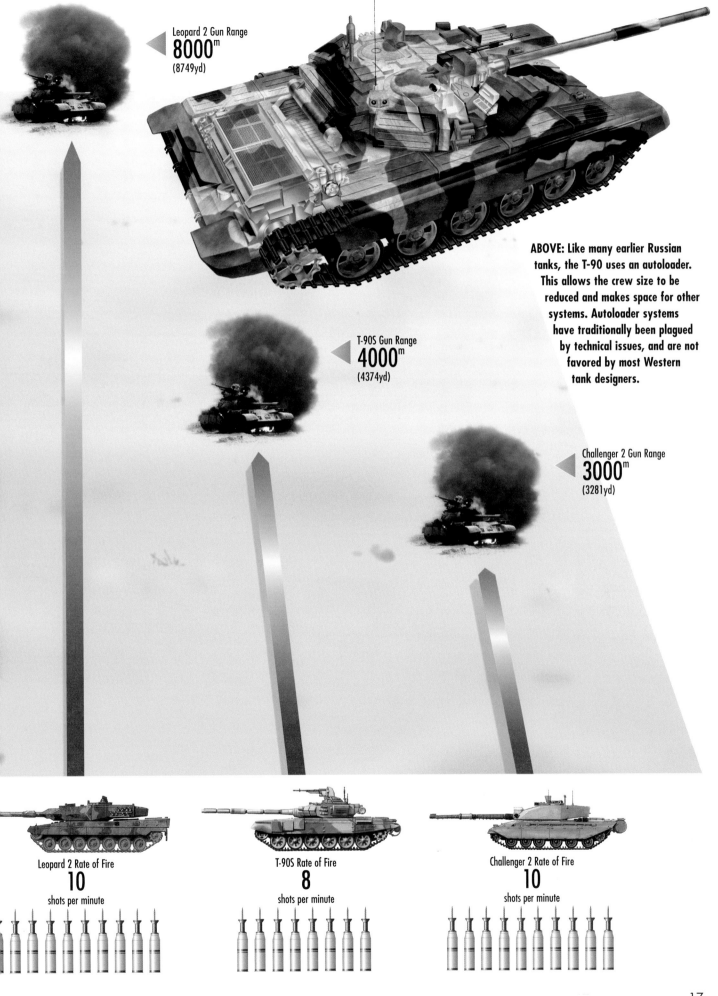

Leopard 2 Gun Range
8000^m
(8749yd)

T-90S Gun Range
4000^m
(4374yd)

Challenger 2 Gun Range
3000^m
(3281yd)

ABOVE: Like many earlier Russian tanks, the T-90 uses an autoloader. This allows the crew size to be reduced and makes space for other systems. Autoloader systems have traditionally been plagued by technical issues, and are not favored by most Western tank designers.

Leopard 2 Rate of Fire
10
shots per minute

T-90S Rate of Fire
8
shots per minute

Challenger 2 Rate of Fire
10
shots per minute

CHAPTER 7

Middle Eastern Main Battle Tanks 1

Operational Range

▶ **Ramses II**
▶ **Merkava**
▶ **Zulfiqar**
▶ **Al-Khalid**

1

Many Middle Eastern tank designs are derived from Russian or Chinese vehicles, often with overseas assistance. Egypt's Ramses II is an updated version of the Russian T-55; the Zulfiqar was developed from the Russian T-72. The Al-Khalid, fielded by Pakistan, was developed in conjunction with China using elements of several earlier Chinese and Russian designs. Developed versions such as these often improve on the originals but also carry forward compromises made in the original design.

The Israeli Merkava series of tanks was developed specifically to meet Israeli needs and to incorporate lessons learned in earlier conflicts. Unusually, it has a front-mounted engine, allowing the hull to incorporate a space at the rear that can be used to carry additional ammunition or even infantry.

The Merkava series has undergone a steady evolution since the Mk 1 was introduced, gaining additional armor, a new engine and weapons, and a lengthened hull. It has come as far from the original design as have many of its Middle Eastern rivals, even if, unlike them, it has retained the original design's name.

Operational range is an important factor in developing or updating a tank design. It does not merely dictate the distance the tank can advance during an offensive, but also indicates how long the tank can go on making small local movements when on the defensive or in close contact with the enemy. Everything a tank does eats up fuel, and a vehicle that runs out is essentially helpless.

OPPOSITE: The Merkava follows an unusual design philosophy. Doors at the rear of the hull allow easy resupply of stores or ammunition, and the tank can carry a squad of infantry in rather cramped safety. In an emergency, the tank can be used to rescue casualties, although this is wasteful of its capabilities.

1 The Israeli Merkava tank was a revolutionary design when it first appeared. Its sloping armor gives excellent protection, and it outguns most other MBTs in the Middle East. It is, however, heavier and slower than most of its adversaries.

Ramses II
600km
(373 miles)

Al-Khalid
450^{km}
(280 miles)

Zulfiqar
500^{km}
(311 miles)

erkava
00^{km}
1 miles)

Operational Range

Operational range is dictated by how much fuel the tank can carry and how fuel-efficient its engine is. High-speed movement or crossing rough terrain increases fuel consumption considerably, which in turn reduces the distance the tank can move before requiring resupply.

Weight

A tank that is too lightly armored will not survive on the battlefield. One whose weapons are inadequate will be ineffectual. Armament and protection are must-haves; designers have more leeway in terms of acceptable speed, and may decide to emphasize combat capability at the expense of pace.

1 Based on the Chinese Type 90-II, the Al-Khalid main battle tank has been developed for use by both the Pakistan and Chinese armed forces.

2 An Israeli Defense Force (IDF) Merkava tank stands watch somewhere in the Golan Heights region.

Zulfiqar Weight
40tonnes
(39.4 tons)

tonnes
40

Zulfiqar Weight: 40 tonnes (39.4 tons)

Ramses II Weight
45.8tonnes
(45.1 tons)

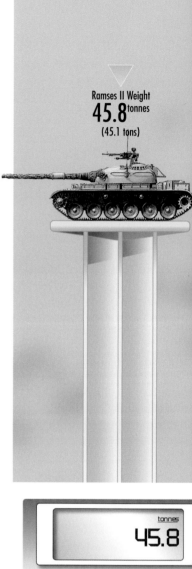

tonnes
45.8

Ramses II Weight: 45.8 tonnes (45.1 tons)

Ramses II Speed
72km/h
(45mph)

Al-Khalid Speed
72km/h
(45mph)

Zulfiqar Speed
70km/h
(43mph)

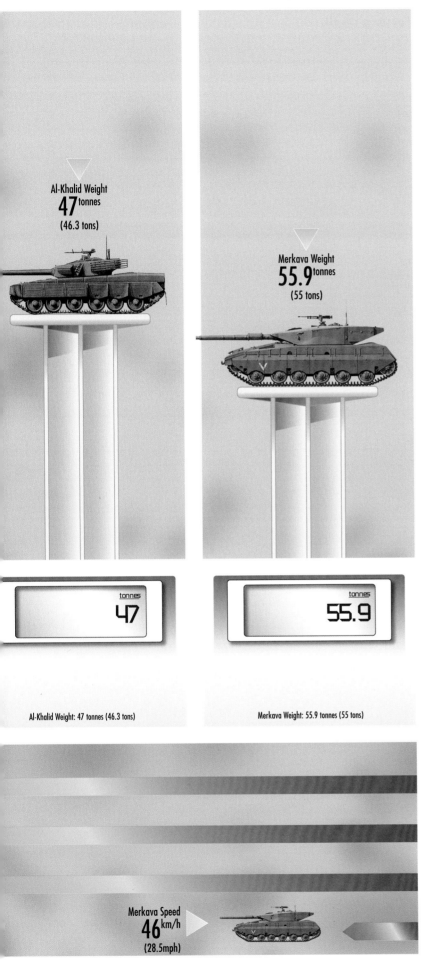

CHAPTER 8

Middle Eastern Main Battle Tanks 2

Weight, Speed and Engine Power

▶ **Ramses II**
▶ **Merkava**
▶ **Zulfiqar**
▶ **Al-Khalid**

To be effective, a tank needs to carry a number of very heavy systems. Its gun and ammunition weigh a lot, and these need a turret with a traversing mechanism capable of supporting them. This, along with the hull, is encased in armor. Making all of this metal move requires a powerful engine that propels the tank via a heavy transmission system and finally the tracks. In order to provide sufficient power, the engine must be large and, inevitably, heavy in weight.

The tank's top speed and its ability to cross rough terrain are both dictated by its weight and the power of its engine. A large engine takes up considerable space inside the tank, and fuel must also be carried; more powerful engines need more fuel to travel the same distance.

If it proves impossible to squeeze a suitable engine into a given hull design, then one solution is to enlarge the hull, but this increases the area that must be armored and thus adds to weight, reducing speed or requiring a larger engine still. A larger engine also adds its own weight to that of the tank – and the cycle continues.

Tank design is always a balancing act between power, weight and space required. Advanced engines with a high power-to-weight ratio offer many advantages, but ultimately any successful main battle tank design will fall within a typical range of power and weight values. There are good reasons why superlight and ultraheavy tanks are not fielded.

Maximum Speed

The Merkava trades mobility for protection, which is acceptable in a design intended mainly for defensive warfare. A relatively heavy (and slow) tank of this type is not well suited to sweeping breakthrough attacks and cannot readily redeploy to meet a new threat or take advantage of an opportunity.

Al-Khalid Weight
47 tonnes
(46.3 tons)

Merkava Weight
55.9 tonnes
(55 tons)

tonnes
47

tonnes
55.9

Al-Khalid Weight: 47 tonnes (46.3 tons)

Merkava Weight: 55.9 tonnes (55 tons)

Merkava Speed
46 km/h
(28.5mph)

Maximum Speed

Top speed is highly important, but it can only be maintained over good ground. Average speed of advance is dictated largely by the ability to cope with obstacles ranging from steep slopes and soft ground to water. All of these are likely to be encountered in a river crossing.

Fording Depth

Tank designers usually build some measure of wading capability into a modern MBT. Without it, operations can be severely restricted by water obstacles. However, deep wading requires specialist equipment such as raised engine intakes, which take up space and add weight to the tank.

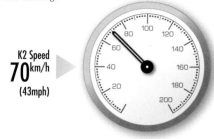

K2 Speed
70km/h
(43mph)

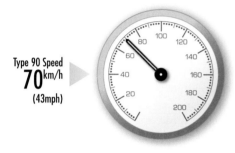

Type 90 Speed
70km/h
(43mph)

Type 90 Fording Depth
2.0m
(6.6ft)

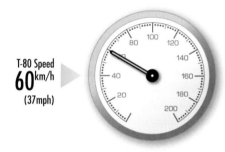

T-80 Speed
60km/h
(37mph)

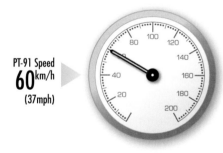

PT-91 Speed
60km/h
(37mph)

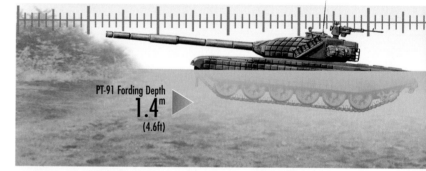

PT-91 Fording Depth
1.4m
(4.6ft)

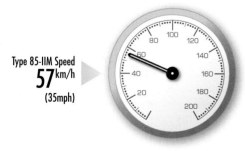

Type 85-IIM Speed
57km/h
(35mph)

Type 85-IIM Fording Depth
1.4m
(4.6ft)

CHAPTER 9

Eastern Main Battle Tanks

Maximum Speed and Fording Depth

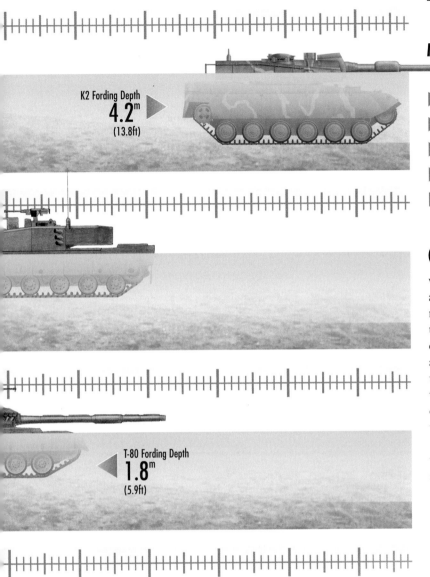

K2 Fording Depth
4.2ᵐ
(13.8ft)

T-80 Fording Depth
1.8ᵐ
(5.9ft)

▶ **Type 85-IIM**
▶ **K2 Black Panther**
▶ **PT-91**
▶ **T-80**
▶ **Type 90 Kyu-maru**

One of the most serious obstacles that can face an armored force is a river or other body of water. For an MBT the only solution is to drive along the bottom. The ability to cross and keep moving is thus defined by the depth of water the tank can successfully negotiate and its ability to cope with underwater obstacles, loose ground and steep banks. In order to ford a river deeper than the bottom of its hull, a tank must be watertight. It must also be able to get air into the engine and exhaust gases out without flooding the engine compartment.

Some tanks must be prepared before entering water, but others, such as the K2 Black Panther, are equipped with a deep-wading kit as standard and can drive straight though any river within their depth capabilities.

BELOW: Developed in China from the unsuccessful Type 85, the Type 85-IIM was given a more powerful gun and an autoloader, plus improved electronics and fire-control systems. It has achieved some export success, with sales to Pakistan.

CHAPTER 10

Infantry Fighting Vehicles of the 90s

Personnel Capacity and Weapons Caliber

▶ **M-60P**

▶ **BTR-80**

▶ **VCC-80 Dardo**

▶ **BTR-90**

▶ **KIVF K-200**

The infantry fighting vehicle (IFV) concept grew out of the armored personnel carrier, but the transition was neither instant nor total. The line between the two remains blurry in places – a lightly armed IFV could arguably be called an APC, whatever classification its designers may give it. In order to provide adequate support for its troop contingent, an IFV needs at least a heavy machine gun and realistically should be armed with an automatic cannon of 20mm (0.79in) or greater caliber.

Some IFVs clearly show their lineage, being little more than upgunned APCs. The M-60P and BTR-80 are examples of this transition. Both are basically armored personnel carriers rather than custom-designed IFVs.

The Korean K-200, on the other hand, was indirectly developed from the immensely successful US M113 APC, but was envisaged from the outset as an IFV. It can ford a shallow river and can also be used as a weapons carrier by adding heavier arms.

Many IFVs incorporate firing ports or even permanently mounted port weapons for troops, which theoretically allows them to fight from inside the vehicle. In practice, it is extremely hard to hit anything from a firing port, and using an IFV as a mobile firing position in this manner is somewhat inefficient. It might be better to replace the troop capacity with a heavier weapon and create a light combat vehicle. After all, an IFV's primary role is still to get infantry where they are going, and infantry, by definition, fight best when dismounted.

Personnel Capacity

The purpose of an IFV remains the same as that of its predecessor, the APC. It is intended to transport infantry quickly to the combat area while protecting them from anti-personnel threats such as snipers, machine guns and artillery-shell fragments.

M-60P

BTR-90

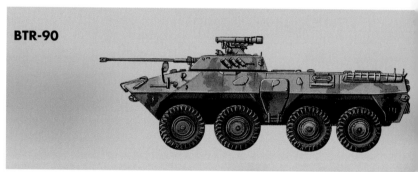

K-200

BTR-80

VCC-80

So long as troop-carrying capacity is not compromised, an IFV should carry as powerful a weapon as possible. The key question is whether to arm it for infantry support with a cannon or machine gun, or to add a missile-based anti-tank capability.

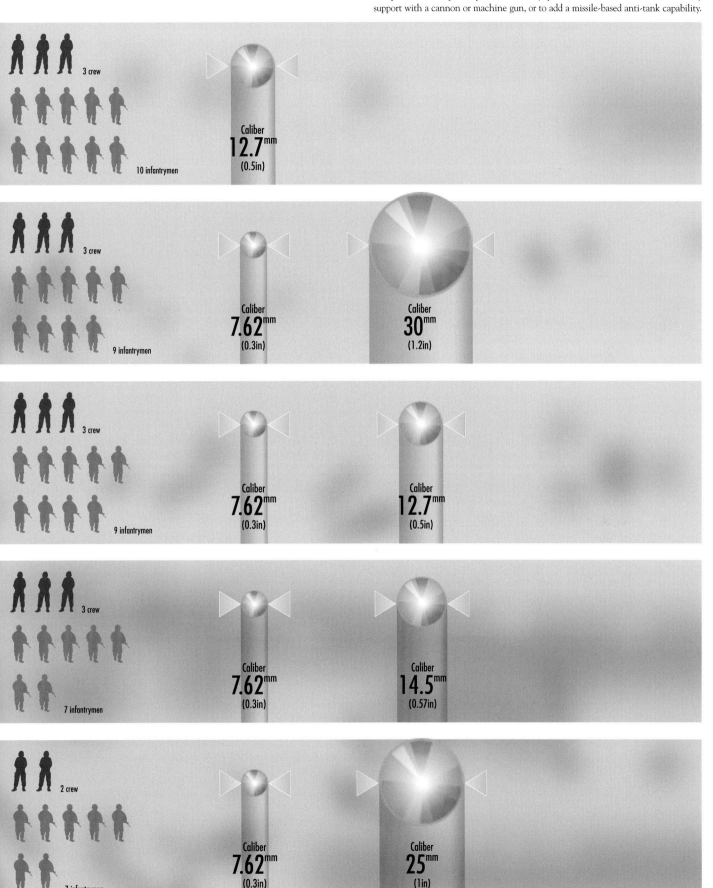

3 crew

10 infantrymen

Caliber
12.7ᵐᵐ
(0.5in)

3 crew

9 infantrymen

Caliber
7.62ᵐᵐ
(0.3in)

Caliber
30ᵐᵐ
(1.2in)

3 crew

9 infantrymen

Caliber
7.62ᵐᵐ
(0.3in)

Caliber
12.7ᵐᵐ
(0.5in)

3 crew

7 infantrymen

Caliber
7.62ᵐᵐ
(0.3in)

Caliber
14.5ᵐᵐ
(0.57in)

2 crew

7 infantrymen

Caliber
7.62ᵐᵐ
(0.3in)

Caliber
25ᵐᵐ
(1in)

Personnel Capacity

The LVTP7 is a specialized vehicle intended to get an assault force ashore against resistance, and to provide light fire support. It was custom-designed with this role in mind, and has a huge troop capacity compared with more conventional IFVs.

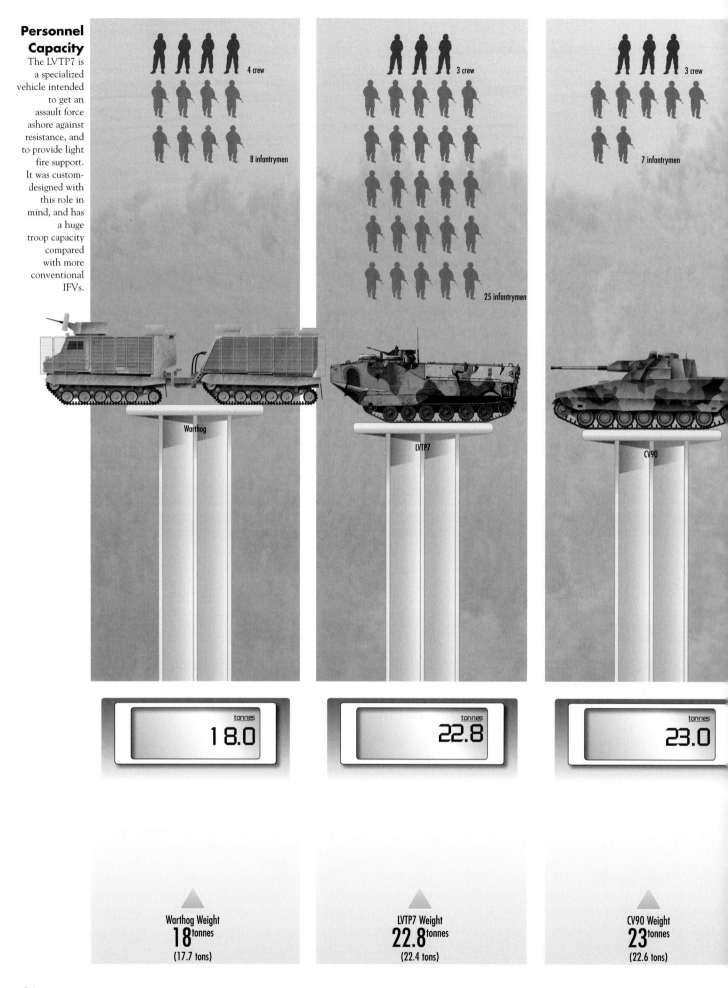

4 crew

8 infantrymen

Warthog

tonnes
18.0

Warthog Weight
18tonnes
(17.7 tons)

3 crew

25 infantrymen

LVTP7

tonnes
22.8

LVTP7 Weight
22.8tonnes
(22.4 tons)

3 crew

7 infantrymen

CV90

tonnes
23.0

CV90 Weight
23tonnes
(22.6 tons)

3 crew

7 infantrymen

Bionix 25

tonnes
23.0

Bionix 25 Weight
23tonnes
(22.6tons)

3 crew

9 infantrymen

Namer

tonnes
60.0

Namer Weight
60tonnes
(59.1 tons)

CHAPTER 11

Tracked Infantry Fighting Vehicles

Weight and Personnel Capacity

▶ **LVTP7**
▶ **CV90**
▶ **Namer**
▶ **Warthog**
▶ **Bionix 25**

A number of innovative IFV designs have emerged in recent years, many of them from the industries of nations such as Singapore. Modern IFVs are designed with more than their immediate capabilities in mind, and often have "growth potential" built into the design. The capacity to be adapted to the needs of an export customer or to accommodate lessons learned during a deployment allows a vehicle to be updated and modified rather than requiring replacement when operational needs change.

Many IFVs are part of a family of variants, which increases their attractiveness to buyers. A single vehicle that can be configured as a weapons carrier, field ambulance, command vehicle or mobile artillery observation post is far more efficient from a maintenance and spares-procurement point of view than several different designs. Thus vehicles such as the Warthog are attractive as they reduce the overall lifetime cost of operating a fleet of light armored vehicles.

Today's IFV designs often use a modular system, allowing armament to be reconfigured as necessary. It is not uncommon for a relatively cheap base model to be offered, along with a number of upgrades and specialist configurations. This brings IFVs within the budget of forces that might otherwise simply not be able to afford them, and in turn increases the potential for export sales. However, custom-designed vehicles such as the US Advanced Amphibious Assault Vehicle (AAAV) are often more effective in their specialist role, making them a good choice for those forces that can afford them.

Weight

The Israeli Namer IFV was created by converting early-model Merkava tanks into personnel carriers. It is very heavy by IFV standards but is also extremely well protected. The weight saved by removing the turret and replacing it with a remotely operated light-weapons mount was used to add greater protection to the hull.

CHAPTER 12
Wheeled Personnel Carriers 1

Maximum Speed

▶ **GTK Boxer**
▶ **LAV III**
▶ **LGS Fennek**
▶ **Stryker**

Tracked vehicles require a great deal of support and maintenance, and are often difficult to deploy quickly or support in difficult conditions. Although their rough-terrain capability is lower, wheeled vehicles are often better suited to rapid-deployment operations. They are also cheaper and arguably better tailored to a peacekeeping or security deployment than a tracked vehicle. Many wheeled personnel carriers are part of a family of vehicles, and in another configuration might be considered a conventional armored car suitable for use in providing fire-support or reconnaissance.

A wheeled APC cannot be as heavily protected as a tracked vehicle due to weight constraints, so will often rely upon speed for protection. The vehicle will be lightly armored and should be able to protect its occupants from machine-gun fire and shell fragments. Many APCs have a secondary layer of protection around the crew area, which prevents small fragments from entering. While this will not help against a direct hit with an anti-tank weapon, it does greatly increase crew survivability against the commonest threats on the modern battlefield, and will usually allow the crew to escape with minor injuries even if the vehicle is disabled.

Successful designs are often used as the basis for further development. Thus the Piranha III, bought by several nations and designated LAV III in Canadian service, was used as the basis for the US Army's Interim Armored Vehicle program and entered service as the Stryker. A fire-support variant with a 105mm (4.1in) gun is built on the same chassis.

RIGHT: A US Army Styker vehicle carries out patrol duties. Wheeled vehicles generally impose less of a logistics burden than tracked equivalents, though they are also usually less capable in combat. The trade-off between more combat vehicles and individual combat capability makes selecting the right armored vehicle a difficult choice.

Maximum Speed
On firm ground or a road, wheeled vehicles are fast compared with tracked equivalents. They are also more fuel efficient, which can be an important consideration when undertaking long-term patrol commitments on a peacekeeping deployment.

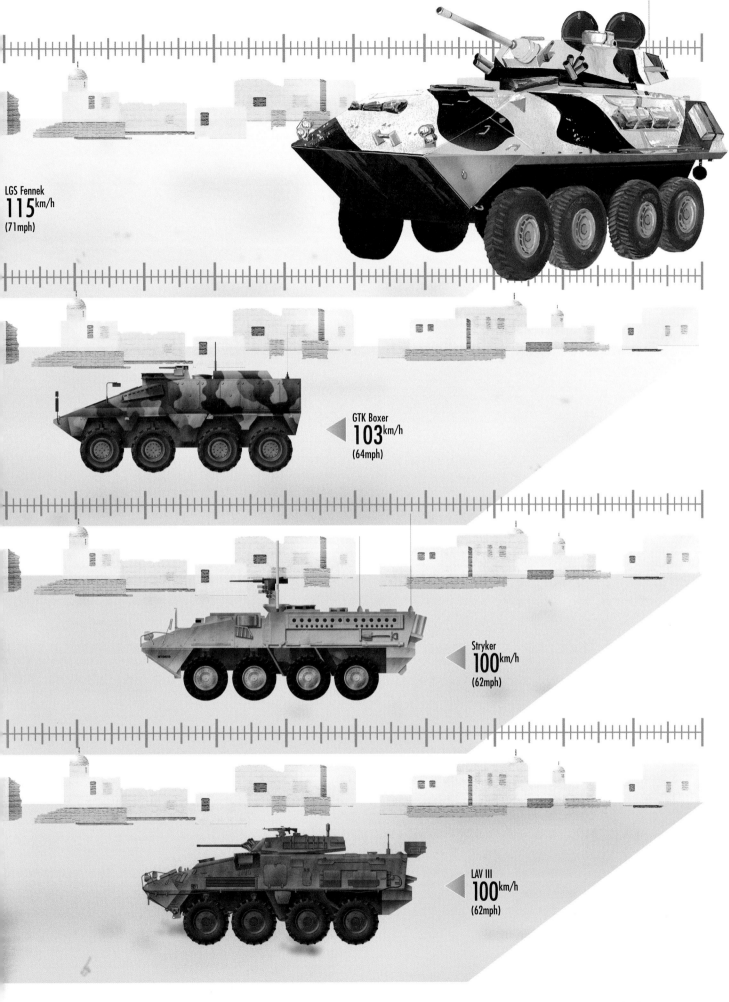

LGS Fennek
115km/h
(71mph)

GTK Boxer
103km/h
(64mph)

Stryker
100km/h
(62mph)

LAV III
100km/h
(62mph)

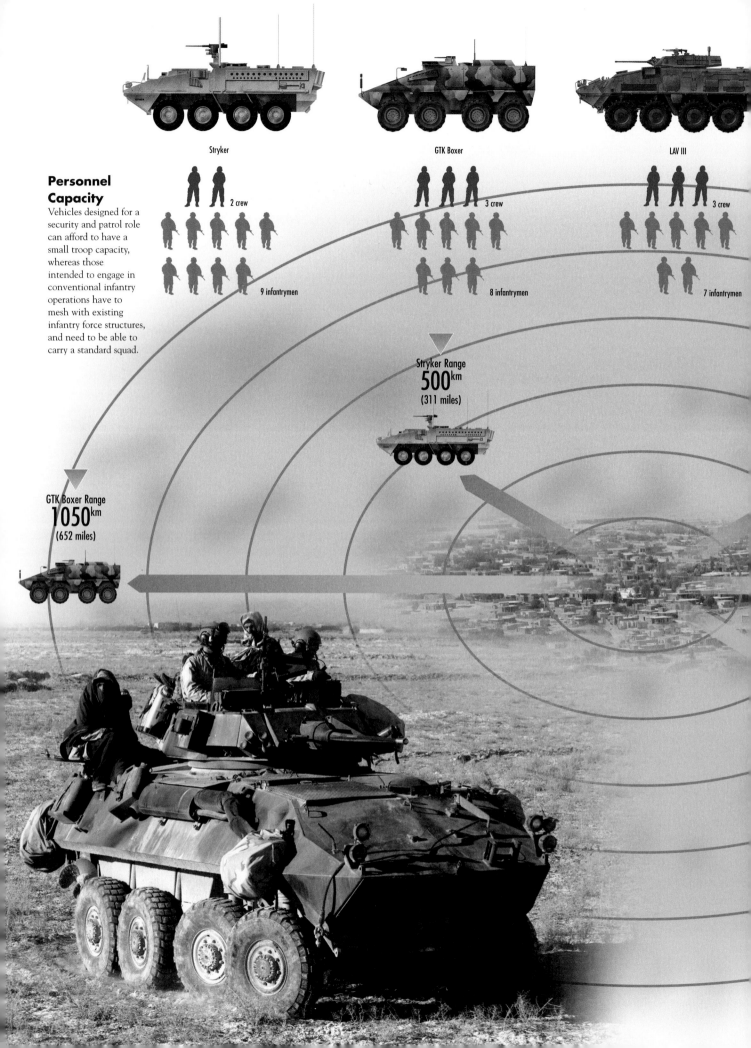

Stryker

GTK Boxer

LAV III

Personnel Capacity

Vehicles designed for a security and patrol role can afford to have a small troop capacity, whereas those intended to engage in conventional infantry operations have to mesh with existing infantry force structures, and need to be able to carry a standard squad.

2 crew

9 infantrymen

3 crew

8 infantrymen

3 crew

7 infantrymen

Stryker Range
500km
(311 miles)

GTK Boxer Range
1050km
(652 miles)

CHAPTER 13

Wheeled Personnel Carriers 2

Operational Range and Personnel Capacity

▶ **GTK Boxer**
▶ **Mastiff PPV**
▶ **LAV III**
▶ **LGS Fennek**
▶ **Stryker**

Mastiff PPV

2 crew

4 infantrymen

LGS Fennek

3 crew

LAV III Range
450km
(280 miles)

Mastiff PPV Range
966km
(600 miles)

LGS Fennek Range
860km
(534 miles)

Operational Range
A large radius of operation is vital to an effective combat vehicle, and even more so if it is to be used for patrol operations. Wheeled APCs are highly useful for security duties, patrolling supply routes and maintaining an "armed presence" across a wide area.

The majority of personnel carriers are designed around the ability to carry an infantry squad or section, of whatever size the owning nation normally deploys. Sometimes design trade-offs force changes of doctrine – for example, smaller squads or a different breakdown of sub-units within a force. In an emergency, such as when only a single vehicle is available to evacuate an infantry force from a dire situation, a surprisingly large number of fully equipped soldiers can be crammed into a small space. This is not conducive to operational efficiency, but it has saved lives.

Some vehicles, such as the Fennek, were designed as reconnaissance assets rather than troop carriers but are sometimes pressed into service to carry a small force when necessary. Others – the Mastiff, for instance – bridge the gap between recce/patrol assets and personnel carriers. The Mastiff was designed as a patrol vehicle that could carry troops, rather than a vehicle to transport troops into combat. It is primarily suited to peacekeeping and security operations, though it can be used as a combat asset at need.

Mines are a major threat to vehicles carrying out relatively predictable patrol operations, such as when on a peacekeeping deployment, and so many modern personnel carriers have excellent mine protection even if their overall armor is not all that heavy. Many wheeled combat vehicles are designed to remain drivable even with a wheel blown off, enabling them to drive out of trouble or to limp home even after serious damage.

OPPOSITE: The LAV III offers a good balance of firepower, transport capacity and mobility. It can serve as a utility supply vehicle at need, or provide security in areas where it is not considered appropriate to deploy tanks. Tracked vehicles are generally seen as more threatening than wheeled ones. Sometimes this is a good thing; when it is not, wheeled vehicles are a better option.

CHAPTER 14

Missile-armed Combat Vehicles

Missile Range

▶ **BTR-90**

▶ **M901**

▶ **VBL**

▶ **M980**

Not all combat vehicles can carry a gun powerful enough to endanger another AFV, but missile systems can be fitted to most vehicles. They are, in general, light and recoilless, so that in theory it is possible to field a vast force of light, highly mobile tank slayers. However, missiles do have drawbacks. They are bulkier than gun rounds, reducing the number of shots available, and are usually expensive. They also produce a lot of backblast, which can reveal a launcher's position.

Despite these drawbacks, many nations field missile-equipped vehicles. They fill a niche once occupied by the gun-armed tank destroyer or the infantry anti-tank gun. Many of the weapons systems in use aboard these vehicles have other applications. The VBL uses MILAN, which is also deployed with infantry formations. This simplifies logistics and training, but infantry missile systems tend to be short-ranged and may lack the capability to destroy a heavily protected MBT.

Heavier missiles such as TOW and Konkurs, as used by the M901 and BTR-90 respectively, use wire-guidance, which allows an accurate attack at a great distance. Their warheads are powerful enough to be effective against most vehicles, but the missile's long flight time makes the launching vehicle vulnerable to return fire. The missile is guided from the vehicle, which must remain halted and exposed while the missile is in flight.

Effective Missile Range
Active guidance makes hitting a moving target at long range a strong possibility, though much depends on the skill of the operator. For a light vehicle engaging tanks, a surprise attack from concealment, ideally at long range, is best as it reduces the chance of effective return fire.

BTR-90
4000ᵐ
(4374yd)

M901
3750ᵐ
(4102yd)

BELOW: Iraqi Army troops speed by in a Soviet-era BPM-1 infantry fighting vehicle. The BMP-1 can carry a 9K32 Strela-2 man-portable anti-aircraft missile launcher.

BTR-90

M901

M980
000ᵐ
(281yd)

M980

VBL
2000ᵐ
(2187yd)

VBL

CHAPTER 15

Big-gun Armored Cars

Maximum Fording Depth, Gradient and Vertical Obstacles

▶ **Rooikat**
▶ **Piranha**
▶ **Renault VBC 90**
▶ **RPX-90**
▶ **Centauro**

The first armored cars were exactly that – ordinary touring cars fitted with some armor and a weapon. Even as the concept matured into a capable combat vehicle, the armored car was still associated with light weapons such as machine guns and automatic cannon. However, advances in technology, especially in recoil control, have made it possible for large armored cars to carry a gun capable of threatening many tanks.

The main problem facing such heavy designs is cross-country mobility. The armored car's main assets are cheapness, compared with tracked AFVs, and high speed. An armored car that is unduly loaded down may lose much of its mobility, and attempts to remedy the problem can drive the cost up to the point where it is just as efficient to deploy tracked vehicles. There is an upper limit to how heavy an armored car can be before it becomes an inferior light tank.

BELOW: The Centauro heavy armored car has proven its worth on peacekeeping operations, where its combination of mobility and heavy firepower makes it ideal for controlling wide areas and protecting supply convoys.

Fording Depth

While some lighter armored car designs are amphibious, most larger models are not. A relatively light weight and buoyant tire can be a disadvantage when trying to gain purchase on a soft riverbed, meaning that armored cars are often less able to ford fast-flowing water than a tracked vehicle of similar size.

Rooikat Fording Depth
1.5ᵐ
(4.9ft)

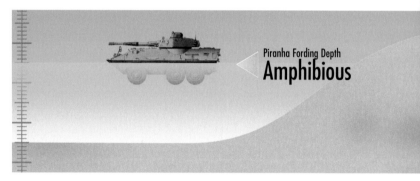

Piranha Fording Depth
Amphibious

Centauro Fording Depth
1.5ᵐ
(4.9ft)

VBC 90 Fording Depth
1.2ᵐ
(3.9ft)

RPX-90 Fording Depth
1.4ᵐ
(4.6ft)

Gradients

Many armored cars have impressive hill-climbing performance. However, traversing a slope is more of a problem. The Rooikat, for example, is challenged by traversing a 30-degree gradient. Anything steeper runs the risk of tipping the vehicle over.

Rooikat Gradient
70%

Rooikat Vertical Obstacle
1.0ᵐ
(3.3ft)

Piranha Gradient
70%

Piranha Vertical Obstacle
0.5ᵐ
(1.6ft)

Centauro Gradient
60%

Centauro Vertical Obstacle
0.55ᵐ
(1.8ft)

VBC 90 Gradient
50%

VBC 90 Vertical Obstacle
0.5ᵐ
(1.6ft)

RPX-90 Gradient
40%

RPX-90 Vertical Obstacle
0.6ᵐ
(2ft)

Vertical Obstacles
The challenge is to deliver enough thrust to force the front wheels up onto the object and to avoid grounding the hull.

Maximum Speed

More wheels means lower ground pressure and better off-road performance once the vehicle exceeds a certain weight, but the wheels and their associated transmission systems also add to the weight of the vehicle, which reduces speed unless a larger engine is fitted.

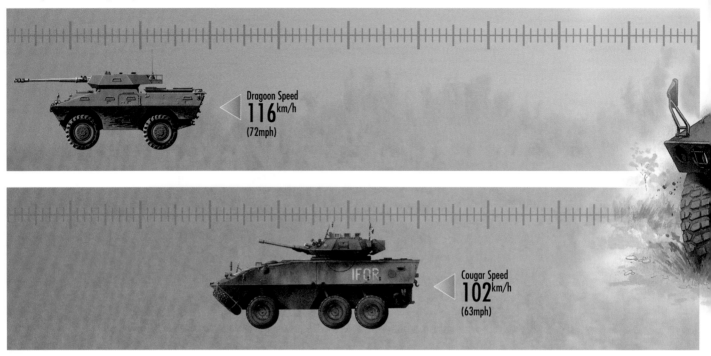

Dragoon Speed
116km/h
(72mph)

Cougar Speed
102km/h
(63mph)

Cascavel Speed
100km/h
(62mph)

ERC 90 Speed
100km/h
(62mph)

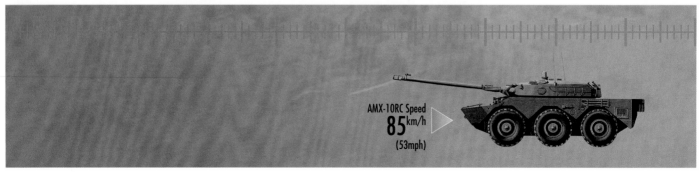

AMX-10RC Speed
85km/h
(53mph)

CHAPTER 16

Fire-support Armored Cars

Maximum Speed and Engine Power

▶ **AMX-10RC**
▶ **Cougar**
▶ **Dragoon**
▶ **ERC 90**
▶ **Engesa EE-9 Cascavel**

A ny armored-vehicle design is a trade-off between armor, firepower and speed, and where a main battle tank emphasizes the first two, armored cars are characterized by speed. If they are also to carry heavy firepower then this must be at the expense of armor protection. As a result, most are protected only against shell splinters and light automatic weapons. Against heavier weapons their best defense is not to be hit, working on the principle that "speed is armor."

Many fire-support armored cars mount a gun in the 90mm (3.5in) category, with some examples using heavier weapons. The Canadian-designed Cougar armored car made use of an existing system by incorporating the entire turret of the Scorpion armored reconnaissance vehicle, including its 76mm (3in) gun. This is quite adequate for fire-support work but insufficient for attacking tanks – the Cougar can fight its own kind but will come off worse in an engagement with anything better protected.

On the other hand, the 105mm (4.1in) gun carried by the French AMX-10RC is capable of penetrating many tanks and offers significantly greater firepower than the more common 90mm (3.5in) gun. However, this comes at a price. Although amphibious and possessing good mobility, the AMX-10RC is significantly slower than many competing designs. Under most circumstances this is not a major drawback, but there are times when high speed can make up for a lack of armor. It is perhaps significant that some of the AMX-10RCs deployed for the Gulf War were up-armored.

Engine Power

A larger and more powerful engine will increase the vehicle's power-to-weight ratio, but it will also increase overall weight and bulk. If the cycle of increased size, power and weight gets out of hand, then an overly large vehicle will be the result; sometimes it is better to accept the lesser capabilities of a small, fast vehicle.

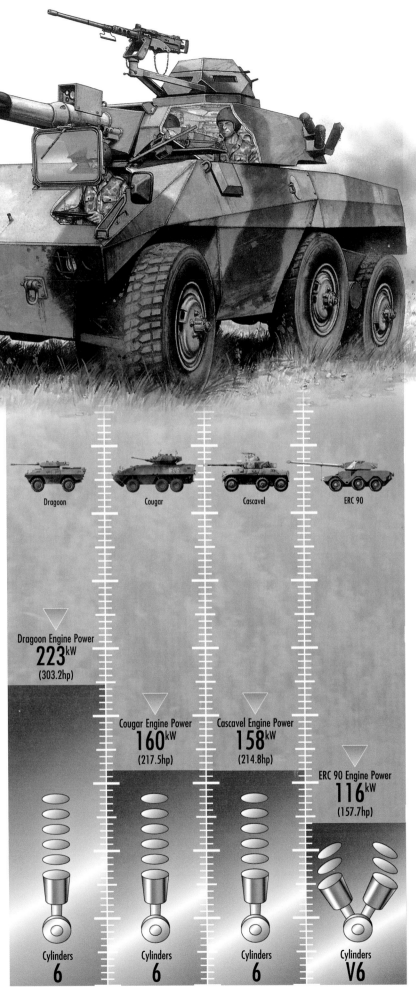

Dragoon   Cougar   Cascavel   ERC 90

Dragoon Engine Power **223**kW (303.2hp)

Cougar Engine Power **160**kW (217.5hp)

Cascavel Engine Power **158**kW (214.8hp)

ERC 90 Engine Power **116**kW (157.7hp)

Cylinders **6**   Cylinders **6**   Cylinders **6**   Cylinders **V6**

CHAPTER 17

Light Tanks and Recce Vehicles 1

Weight vs Maximum Speed

- ▶ **VEC Cavalry Scout Vehicle**
- ▶ **OTO Melara R3 Capraia**
- ▶ **FV107 Scimitar**
- ▶ **Scorpion 90**
- ▶ **Stingray 2**

Speed and mobility are the primary assets of reconnaissance vehicles, enabling them to avoid contact with the enemy wherever possible. However, light vehicles of this sort are also highly useful as a source of rapidly deployable firepower. They are thus often used as the "teeth" of fast-moving cavalry formations and to add firepower to an infantry force. Their small size and relatively low weight enables light vehicles to be transported by air and, in some cases, even dropped by parachute.

There are times when light armored vehicles are the only ones available, and as a rule any armored support is better than no armored support. Thus for rapid-deployment forces or those operating in very distant areas, light vehicles are a good option. Weight and overall size become very important considerations when loading an amphibious warfare ship or a transport aircraft.

A variety of approaches are taken by light-armored-vehicle designers, and there is no clear point where wheels or tracks are "better." The choice depends on a range of factors, including the sort of terrain the vehicle may have to operate in, the availability of good maintenance and support, and whether strategic or tactical mobility is more important. Experience has shown that there are places that a light tank such as a Scorpion or Scimitar can go that even infantry will struggle to get across. A wheeled vehicle would not be able to cope with such terrain, but on firmer ground a wheeled vehicle can travel faster for longer.

Weight

The acceptable weight of a vehicle depends upon what it is designed to do. The Scorpion and Scimitar were both intended primarily for the armored reconnaissance role, whereas the Stingray is more of a combat or fire-support platform, and requires heavier armament and protection.

Capraia Speed
120km/h
(75mph)

Capraia

Scimitar Speed
80km/h
(50mph)

Scimitar

tonnes
3.2

Capraia Weight
3.2tonnes
(3.1 tons)

tonnes
7.8

Scimitar Weight
7.8tonnes
(7.7 tons)

Maximum Speed

There is a fairly obvious correlation between weight and maximum speed, with the choice of wheels or tracks further affecting the equation. Although a wheeled vehicle of a given weight will have a higher top speed than a tracked vehicle, average speed overland can be lower depending on the terrain.

Scorpion 90 Speed
73km/h
(45.5mph)

VEC Speed
103km/h
(64mph)

Stingray 2 Speed
69km/h
(43mph)

Scorpion 90

VEC

Stingray 2

tonnes
8.6

tonnes
13.8

tonnes
19.1

Scorpion 90 Weight
8.6tonnes
(8.5 tons)

VEC Weight
13.8tonnes
(13.6 tons)

Stingray 2 Weight
19.1tonnes
(18.8 tons)

CHAPTER 18

Light Tanks and Recce Vehicles 2

Operational Range and Weapons Caliber

▶ **VEC Cavalry Scout Vehicle**
▶ **OTO Melara R3 Capraia**
▶ **FV107 Scimitar**
▶ **Scorpion 90**
▶ **Stingray 2**

The uses that light armored vehicles are put to depends greatly upon what other weapons systems are available. Often there is no choice but to fight with whatever is at hand, but if "real" tanks can reach the combat area quickly enough then light assets are better used for flank protection and reconnaissance. In the former role, the high speed of light tanks is a great advantage as they can move to counter any attempt to get around the flank of the main force, if necessary fighting a highly fluid delaying action while heavier assets redeploy to deal with the threat.

In order to keep their weight down and make them small targets, some light armored vehicles use a relatively light weapon or a gun-over-hull configuration. The latter is an unarmored weapon mounting controlled from within the vehicle, dispensing with the weight of a turret and its associated armor. A hit on the weapon will probably disable it, but the chances of being hit or even spotted are minimized by reducing the overall size of the vehicle.

Many light tanks are designed for the export market, and as such may be fitted into a variety of roles by the end user. The Stingray, for example, mounts a 105mm (4.1in) gun that enables its use as a light battle tank if necessary. It is really too lightly armored for this role, but in some parts of the world it will not encounter first-line anti-tank weapons. In such an environment a relatively cheap vehicle may be able to fill in for heavier tanks without being excessively vulnerable.

Operational Range

Armored reconnaissance often requires quite long forays into potentially hostile territory, and sometimes a rapid retreat becomes necessary. Operational range is calculated on the basis of a modest speed, but long range can translate into the ability to flee at top speed for a lengthy period. While undignified, this is a survival trait in a reconnaissance vehicle.

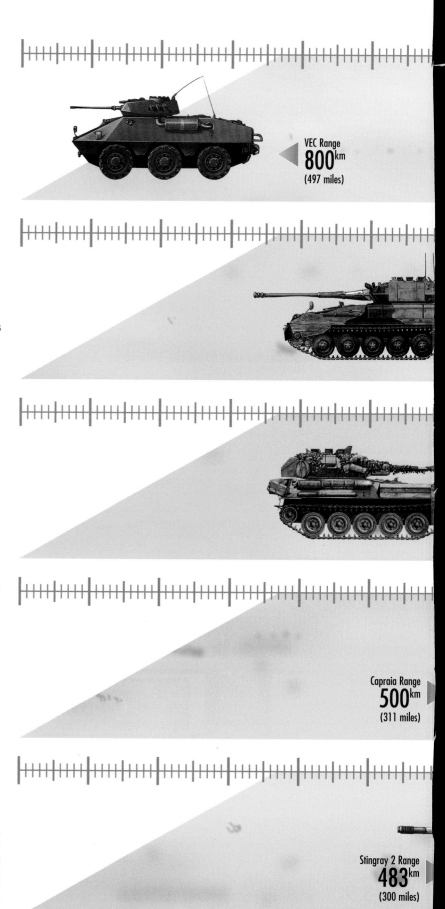

VEC Range
800km
(497 miles)

Capraia Range
500km
(311 miles)

Stingray 2 Range
483km
(300 miles)

Weapons Caliber

The most important "weapon" aboard a reconnaissance vehicle is probably its radio; information gathered allows more powerful assets to be brought to bear. However, an effective weapons system is important to any vehicle likely to be in proximity to the enemy.

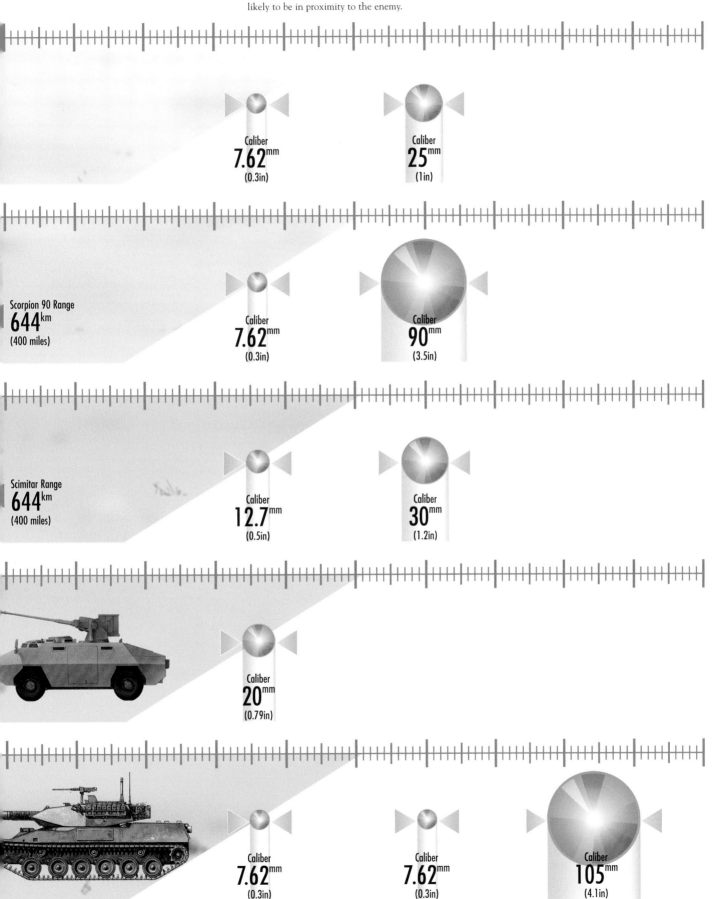

Caliber
7.62mm
(0.3in)

Caliber
25mm
(1in)

Scorpion 90 Range
644km
(400 miles)

Caliber
7.62mm
(0.3in)

Caliber
90mm
(3.5in)

Scimitar Range
644km
(400 miles)

Caliber
12.7mm
(0.5in)

Caliber
30mm
(1.2in)

Caliber
20mm
(0.79in)

Caliber
7.62mm
(0.3in)

Caliber
7.62mm
(0.3in)

Caliber
105mm
(4.1in)

Maximum Speed

A high road speed is important for patrol vehicles. Lacking significant armor, mobility is their best defense, and the ability to react rapidly to a situation developing some distance away is essential to maintaining control over an area.

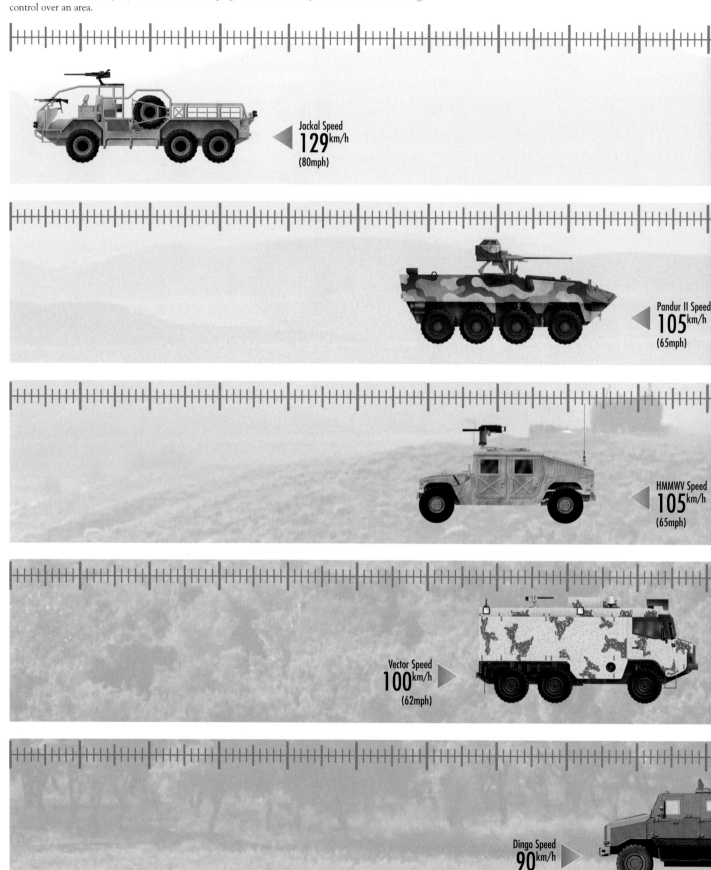

Jackal Speed
129km/h
(80mph)

Pandur II Speed
105km/h
(65mph)

HMMWV Speed
105km/h
(65mph)

Vector Speed
100km/h
(62mph)

Dingo Speed
90km/h
(56mph)

CHAPTER 19

Multi-purpose Patrol Vehicles 1

Maximum Speed and Weight

▶ **M998 HMMWV**
▶ **AFT Dingo**
▶ **Jackal MWMIK**
▶ **Pandur II**
▶ **Pinzgauer Vector PPV**

Jackal Weight
6.7 tonnes
(6.6 tons)

tonnes
6.7

Pandur II Weight
15 tonnes
(14.8 tons)

tonnes
15.0

HMMWV Weight
3.9 tonnes
(3.8 tons)

tonnes
3.9

Vector Weight
6.6 tonnes
(6.5 tons)

tonnes
6.6

Dingo Weight
11.9 tonnes
(11.7 tons)

tonnes
11.9

In the post–Cold War world, there is still a need for heavy armored forces and their supporting arms – self-propelled artillery and infantry fighting vehicles. However, these systems are extremely expensive and are not well suited to routine patrol and security operations. Heavy forces are best kept concentrated to deal with major threats or to crush opposition, leaving security work to lighter vehicles.

A large part of any modern military operation is security work. This includes protection of rear areas and lines of supply, but also the seemingly endless patrolling required to establish and maintain control over the countryside. Often, opposition forces are dispersed, and will try to influence an area or cause the security forces to lose control rather than engage in a direct large-scale confrontation that they will probably lose. A series of fleeting contacts is more likely than a set-piece battle, and the equipment required is rather different.

Light patrol vehicles are inexpensive enough that they can be deployed in fairly large numbers. Many use components from commercial vehicles, which reduces overall costs significantly. Carrying a support weapon such as a machine gun and a small group of infantry personnel, these light vehicles allow the security forces to maintain a presence over a wide area and to rush additional troops into the vicinity of any contact that occurs. Since they commonly operate in areas with poor infrastructure, patrol vehicles need to be relatively light in order to use local bridges and poor roads.

Weight

Many patrol vehicles are based on or developed from light civilian off-road trucks. Although they carry little protection compared with combat vehicles, adding armor increases the vehicle's weight significantly and often requires a redesigned chassis and/or suspension system.

CHAPTER 20

Multi-purpose Patrol Vehicles 2

Operational Range and Personnel Capacity

▶ **M998 HMMWV**
▶ **AFT Dingo**
▶ **Jackal MWMIK**
▶ **Pandur II**
▶ **Pinzgauer Vector PPV**

Most patrol vehicles are resistant to small-arms fire and fragmentation but not to heavier weapons. While it is always desirable to provide the best possible protection, this must be balanced against vehicle weight and troop capacity. Design philosophies regarding the latter vary considerably, depending largely on the role envisaged for the vehicle and its troop complement.

In some cases the vehicle itself is the main asset, acting as an armed presence and mobile eyes. Vehicles such as the HMMWV and Jackal, with a very small troop capacity, fall into this category. As a weapons carrier with a couple of infantrymen in the back, a vehicle of this sort is a potent force in the local area but is limited in some ways. If it is desirable to send a ground force into an area inaccessible to the vehicle then additional personnel must be brought in by other means or several vehicles tasked as transport. Of course, in the latter case this does mean that the infantry force will be very well supported if combat begins.

With larger-capacity vehicles such as the Pandur or Dingo, the infantry force is the main asset and the vehicle acts as transport. Vehicles of this sort are better suited to deploying small foot patrols, which can enter a village or an area normally inaccessible to vehicles. The vehicle's support weapons will not be far away, but locals who are inclined to be friendly are more likely to interact with infantry personnel than with the crew of a heavily armed vehicle.

Personnel Capacity

Even a relatively small vehicle represents a significant investment for the owning force, and needs to be well suited to its task. A design such as the Pandur is essentially a light armored personnel carrier; the HMMWV, however, represents a rather different approach to the problem.

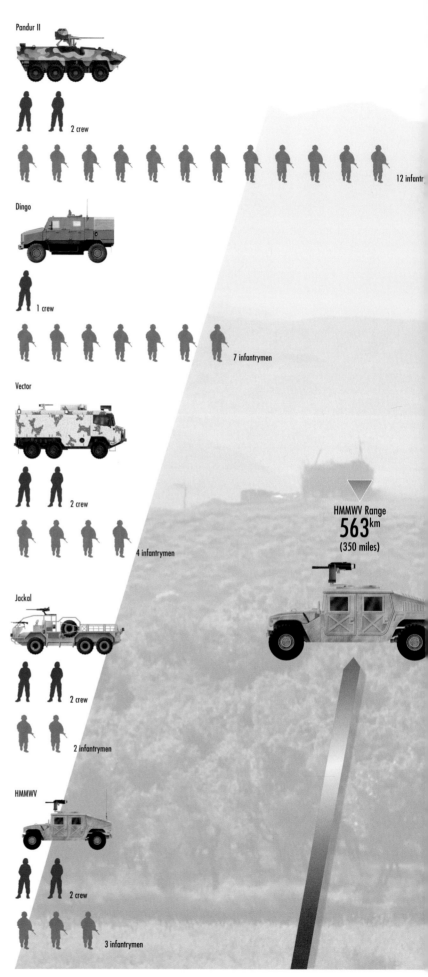

Pandur II

2 crew

12 infantr

Dingo

1 crew

7 infantrymen

Vector

2 crew

4 infantrymen

Jackal

2 crew

2 infantrymen

HMMWV

2 crew

3 infantrymen

HMMWV Range
563km
(350 miles)

Dingo Range
1000km
(621 miles)

Jackal Range
800km
(497 miles)

Pandur II Range
600km
(373 miles)

Vector Range
400km
(249 miles)

1 Iraqi Army soldiers undergo training with a HMMWV.
2 A US Army M998 HMMWV stands watch somewhere in Iraq, 2004.

1

2

Operational Range

Patrolling eats up fuel at a surprisingly high rate. A vehicle that moves its troop complement to their area of operations, then waits for them to complete a foot patrol, will be able to undertake longer patrols than one that is expected to function as a mobile patrol/ reconnaissance asset.

Glossary

adversary An opponent in a conflict.

amphibious Suited for both land and water; involving forces landed from the sea.

armament Military weapons and equipment.

armored personnel carrier (APC) An armored vehicle that is usually armed with machine guns and that transports infantry to the battle before the troops dismount to fight on their own.

assets Military equipment, such as planes, ships, communications and radar installations, employed or targeted in military operations.

breech The part of a cannon behind the bore or the back part of a rifle or gun barrel.

chassis The base frame of a motor vehicle or other wheeled means of transportation.

composite armor The type of vehicle armor that is made up of layers of different material such as metals, plastics and ceramics and that is generally used to cover warships, tanks and fortifications.

conducive Making a certain situation or outcome likely or possible.

contingent A body of troops sent to join a larger force in an operation.

deployment The movement of troops into a position for military action.

dismount To get off or down from something.

foray A sudden attack into enemy territory; a raid.

hull The main body of a vessel or vehicle.

infantry fighting vehicle (IVF) A heavily armed and armored combat vehicle that has tracks or wheels and that is used to transport infantry into battle and to support troops there.

logistics The organization of moving, housing and supplying troops and equipment.

muzzle The open end of the barrel of a firearm.

potent Having great power or effect.

protracted Lasting for a long time or longer than expected or usual.

recce Slang for "reconnaissance."

recoil To move abruptly backward as a reaction on firing a bullet, shell or other missile.

reconnaissance Military observation of a region to locate an enemy or discern strategic features.

sabot A device that ensures the correct positioning of a bullet or shell in the barrel of a gun, attached either to the projectile or inside the barrel and falling away as it leaves the muzzle.

smoothbore gun A gun with an unrifled barrel; in other words, a gun that does not have internal spiral grooves inside the barrel.

suspension The system of springs and shock absorbers by which a vehicle is cushioned from road conditions.

tracked vehicle A vehicle with a continuous interlocking metal band around its wheels, such as that in heavy vehicles like tanks and bulldozers, which enables movement over rough or soft ground.

traversing mechanism A mechanism by which a gun or other device can be turned in a horizontal plane.

turret A low, flat armored gun emplacement that usually revolves, as that in a ship, aircraft, or tank.

For More Information

American Armored Foundation Tank Museum
3401 U.S. Highway 29B
Danville, VA 24540
(434) 836-5323
Web site: http://www.aaftankmuseum.com
The tank museum collects, restores, preserves and exhibits military tanks and artifacts from all time periods and nations.

American Military Museum
The Whittier Narrows Recreation Area
1918 Rosemead Boulevard
South El Monte, CA 91733
(626) 442-1776
Web site: http://www.tankland.com
This museum collects, preserves, restores and exhibits military equipment.

Military Vehicle Technology Foundation
P.O. Box 7390
Menlo Park, CA 94026
Web site: http://www.mvtf.org
This foundation oversees one of the largest collections of historical military vehicles in the world. It also maintains a large technical library that describes vehicle parts and workings. It covers the technology and history of tanks, missile launchers, armored vehicles, field artillery, reconnaissance vehicles, self-propelled guns, engines, firearms and ordnance.

The Tank Museum
Bovington
Dorset BH20 6JG
United Kingdom
01929 405096
Web site: http://www.tankmuseum.org
This British museum covers the story of the tank and tank crews covering about 100 years.

U.S. Army Center of Military History
Fort Lesley J. McNair
Washington, DC 20319-5058
Web site: http://www.history.army.mil
This center records the official history of the army in both peace and war.

World Tank Museum
2625 Alcatraz Avenue #237
Berkeley, CA 94705
(510) 869-9941
Web Site: http://www.world-tank-museum.com
This Web site offers detailed model replicas of historical tanks and armored fighting vehicles.

Web Sites

Due to the changing nature of Internet links, Rosen Publishing has developed an online list of Web sites related to the subject of this book. This site is updated regularly. Please use this link to access the list:

http://www.rosenlinks.com/MODW/Armo

For Further Reading

Bishop, Chris. *The Encyclopedia of Tanks and Armored Fighting Vehicles: From World War I to the Present Day*. San Diego, CA: Thunder Bay Press, 2006.
Bradford, George. *Allied Armored Fighting Vehicles* (World War II AFV Plans). Mechanicsburg, PA: Stackpole Books, 2009.
Bradford, George. *Axis Armored Fighting Vehicles* (World War II AFV Plans). Mechanicsburg, PA: Stackpole Books, 2009.
Bradford, George. *American Armored Fighting Vehicles* (World War II AFV Plans). Mechanicsburg, PA: Stackpole Books, 2007.
Bradford, George. *Russian Armored Fighting Vehicles* (Word War II AFV Plans). Mechanicsburg, PA: Stackpole Books, 2007.
Colson, Rob Scott. *Tanks and Military Vehicles* (Ultimate Machines). London, UK: Wayland, 2012.
Forty, George, and Jack Livesey. *The Complete Guide to Tanks & Armored Fighting Vehicles*. Wigston, UK: Anness, 2012.
Foss, Chistopher F. *Janes' Tank Recognition Guide*. 4th ed. New York, NY: HarperCollins, 2006.
Hama, Larry, and Bill Cain. *Tank of Tomorrow: Stryker* (High-Tech Military Weapons). New York, NY: Children's Press, 2007.
Haskew, Michael. *Postwar Armored Fighting Vehicles: 1945–Present* (Essential Vehicle Identification Guides). Phoenix, AZ: Amber, 2010.
Haskew, Michael E. *Tanks: Inside & Out* (Weapons of War). New York, NY: Rosen Publishing Group, Inc., 2012.
Jackson, Robert. *Tanks and Armored Fighting Vehicles: Visual Encyclopedia*. Edison, NJ: Chartwell Books, Inc., 2012.
Jackson, Robert, ed. *101 Great Tanks* (The 101 Greatest Weapons of All Times). New York, NY: Rosen Publishing Group, Inc., 2010.
Livesey, Jack. *Modern Armored Fighting Vehicles: From 1946 to the Present Day*. Wigston, UK: Anness, 2008.

Index

About the Author

Martin J. Dougherty is a writer and editor specializing in military and defense topics. He is an expert on asymmetric and nonconventional warfare. His published works deal with subjects ranging from naval weapons to personal security. He is the author of *Small Arms Visual Encyclopedia*, *Tanks of World War II*, and *Essential Weapons Identification Guide: Small Arms: 1945–Present*.